A Walk in the Tundra

by Rebecca L. Johnson

with illustrations by Phyllis V. Saroff

HAMPTON-BROWN

THE EXCHANGE

Is it important to care about faraway places? Why or why not?

For my niece Claire, who
helps me see the world with
fresh eyes

             -R. L. J.

A Walk in the Tundra by Rebecca L. Johnson, illustrated by Phyllis V. Saroff.
Text copyright © 2001 by Rebecca L. Johnson. Illustrations copyright © 2001
by Phyllis V. Saroff. This edition is published by Hampton-Brown, by
arrangement with Carolrhoda Books, Inc., a division of Lerner Publishing
Group, 241 First Avenue North, Minneapolis, MN 55401 U.S.A.

On-Page Coach ™ (introductions, questions, on-page glossaries), The Exchange,
back cover summary © Hampton-Brown.

Hampton-Brown
P.O. Box 223220
Carmel, California 93922
800-333-3510
www.hampton-brown.com

Printed in the United States of America

ISBN-13: 978-0-7362-2798-8
ISBN-10: 0-7362-2798-9

2 3 4 5 6 7 8 9 10 19 18 17 16 15 14 13

Words to Know

ALGAE (AL-Jee)—tiny, plant-like living things

ARCTIC—the cold region around the North Pole, north of the Arctic Circle

BACTERIA (bak-TEE-ree-uh)—microscopic, one-celled living things found almost everywhere

BIOME (BYE-ohm)—a major community of living things that covers a large area, such as a grassland or a forest

CLIMATE (KLYE-mut)—a region's usual pattern of weather over a long period of time

CYGNETS (SIG-nets)—baby swans

DISGUISE (dis-GIZE)—something that hides a living thing's true identity

EXTINCT—no longer living on Earth

FUNGI (FUHN-gye)—living things such as mushrooms or molds that get their food by breaking down dead plant and animal matter

LICHEN (LYE-ken)—small, crusty living things made up of fungi and algae growing together

PERMAFROST (PUR-muh-frawst)—permanently frozen ground

POLLEN—fine, powdery material made by flowers. Pollen is usually yellow.

PREDATORS (PREH-duh-turz)—animals that hunt and eat other animals

PREY (pray)—animals that are hunted and eaten by other animals

SHRUB—a low-growing plant with woody stems and branches

TUNDRA—a cold, treeless plain near the top of the world

Far north, near the top of the world, is an area called the tundra. Most of the year the tundra is very cold and dark. But during the short summer, the sun shines day and night.

Cold wind

across the arctic tundra

Overhead, a snowy owl **soars** through the pale blue sky. Spring sunlight glows on her **broad** white wings.

Something small and furry moves in the grass. The owl **swoops**. She catches a lemming in her long, sharp claws. But this food is not for her. The owl has hungry chicks to feed. With the lemming in her beak, she spreads her wings and flies off across the arctic tundra.

soars flies
broad wide
swoops flies to the ground

In some places on the tundra, rolling hills rise to rugged slopes (above). Other parts of the tundra are almost flat (right).

Tundra. The word sounds like the place. It's lonely, windy, and cold. There isn't a tree **in sight**, just **mile after mile of empty plain**. The arctic tundra is so wide and open it seems as if the land could swallow the sky.

Where is the tundra? If you fly south from the North Pole, arctic tundra is the first land you see. It covers the northern parts of **all the continents that surround the top of the world**. In North America, tundra stretches from the Arctic Ocean south to the middle of Canada.

---

in sight anywhere
mile after mile of empty plain many miles of land without trees
all the continents that surround the top of the world North America, Europe, and Asia

Biomes of North America

Arctic Ocean

Atlantic Ocean

Pacific Ocean

Legend:
- tundra
- boreal forest
- deciduous forest
- temperate rain forest
- grassland
- desert
- chaparral
- tropical rain forest
- tropical scrub forest

As you keep flying south, the landscape changes. You pass over dark green forests. Later you see **rolling grasslands** and dry deserts. Tundra, forests, grasslands, and deserts **make up** Earth's main **land zones**. Scientists call these different land zones biomes.

....

rolling grasslands large areas of flat, grassy land

make up are

land zones types of land

Each biome has a different type of climate. The climate is an area's usual pattern of weather over a long period of time.

Every biome is home to a special group of plants. The plants are **well suited to** living in that climate and to growing in the soil found there.

Every biome is also home to a special group of animals. In one way or another, the animals depend on the plants to survive. Many of a biome's animals eat plants. Other animals eat the plant-eaters.

Purple saxifrage is well suited to survive the tundra's harsh climate. It is one of the first plants to bloom each spring.

---

well suited to comfortable

BEFORE YOU MOVE ON...

1. **Viewing** Look at the map on page 8. What does it tell you about the tundra?

2. **Greek and Latin Roots** The Greek word *bio* means *life*. What is a *biome*?

LOOK AHEAD Read pages 10–15 to find out about the climate in the tundra.

9

In winter, temperatures drop far below zero on the tundra.

All the plants and animals in a biome form a community. In that community, every living thing depends on other community members to survive. A biome's climate, soil, plants, and animals are all connected this way.

The arctic tundra has a cold, dry, harsh climate. From September through May, the tundra is **locked in winter's icy grip**. The ground is frozen as hard as stone. Snow **sweeps** across the land, **driven by howling winds**.

....

locked in winter's icy grip very cold
sweeps blows
driven by howling winds blown by fast winds

Tundra animals, such as these musk oxen, must endure long, bitterly cold winters.

Winter days are short. The nights are very long. In the tundra's far north, the sun doesn't come up at all **at midwinter**. It is dark both night and day.

---

at midwinter in the middle of the winter

The winter sun sets on the snow-covered tundra.

Tundra summers last just three months, from June through August. But summer days on the tundra are long and sunny. The sun shines both day and night. Midnight is nearly as bright as noon.

This photo shows how the sun moves above the horizon, hour by hour, during a summer night at the edge of the Arctic Ocean.

In summer, temperatures may get above 50°F. But frost is still possible in July.

100° F
90°
80°
70°
60°
50°
40°
30°
20°
10°
0°
-10°
-20°
-30°
-40°
-50°
-60°

13

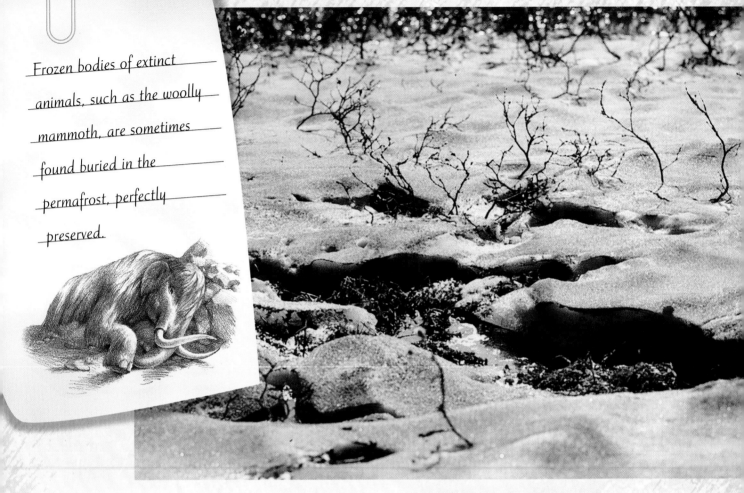

Frozen bodies of extinct animals, such as the woolly mammoth, are sometimes found buried in the permafrost, perfectly preserved.

At the beginning of the summer, sunshine and warmer temperatures melt the snow that winter left behind. But because summer is so short, only the top few inches of soil **thaw out**. Deeper down, the ground never thaws. This ground that is always frozen is called permafrost.

thaw out warm up

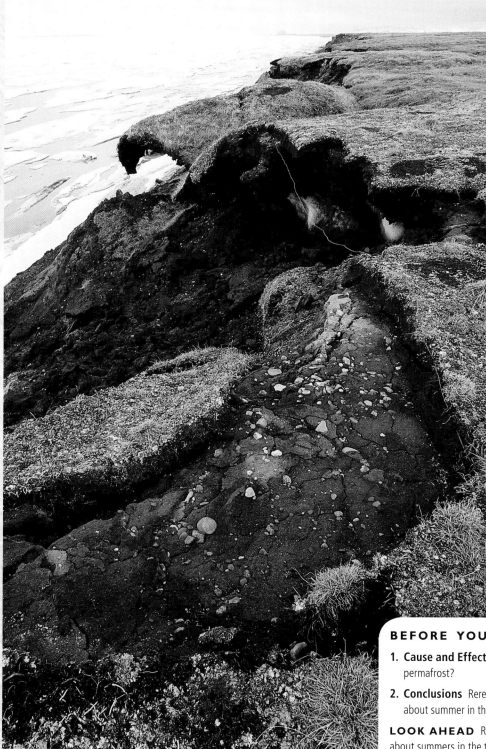

Spring sunlight begins to melt the snow (left). Where the tundra meets the sea, you can see permafrost underneath the top layers of soil (right).

BEFORE YOU MOVE ON...

1. **Cause and Effect** Why does the tundra have permafrost?

2. **Conclusions** Reread page 12. What is unusual about summer in the tundra?

LOOK AHEAD Read pages 16–25 to find out about summers in the tundra.

Tundra summers are short but busy. The snow melts
and plants hurry to grow and bloom.

Tender shoots push up through damp tundra soil in spring (left). On high ground (below), white tufts of cotton grass sway in the cool summer breeze. Shallow pools cover the tundra in lower areas.

It is early summer. The breeze is cool, but the sun is warm. Let's take a walk on the tundra. We can see what life is like in this biome near the top of the world.

The **surface** of the tundra is **getting soggy** as it thaws. Feel how **squishy** the ground is beneath your feet? Because of the permafrost, water can't soak into the ground.

....

surface top
getting soggy becoming soft and wet
squishy soft

Constant freezing and melting make tundra ground lumpy and cracked and hard to walk on.

The water **collects** in low spots. There, it forms shallow lakes and ponds. Parts of the tundra **are dotted with** these pools of water for most of the summer. Yet it rarely rains. So on higher ground, the soil can get very dry.

....

collects stays
are dotted with have many of

Most tundra plants have shallow roots. Roots can't grow into permafrost.

Poke your finger into the soil at your feet. It is cold, gritty, and damp. Just a few inches down, it's **frozen solid**. Worms, fungi, and bacteria **break down** dead plant and animal matter that collects on the ground. They turn it into soil. The soil feeds the plants and helps them to grow. But because the tundra soil is always quite cold, fungi and bacteria here work very, very slowly.

···

Poke Push
frozen solid completely frozen
break down change the

Low-growing tundra plants bloom in a rainbow of colors during the short summer.

So the soil is thin and **poor**. It contains only a little bit of what tundra plants need to grow well.

As you walk along, notice how short the plants are. Few grow **more than knee-high**. Tundra plants **hug** the ground to escape the fierce winds. They form a **dense mat** that covers the land like a thick carpet.

....

poor not good for growing anything

more than knee-high higher than your knee

hug grow close to

dense mat thick covering

Clumps of soft moss grow along the banks of a stream. White anemone (bottom right) and tiny campion flowers (top right) bloom just inches above the ground.

Bend down for a closer look. You'll see mosses, grasses, and wildflowers. **Run your fingers over** a patch of moss. Its dark green surface is velvety soft.

Many different kinds of plants grow on the tundra. They are all crowded together. Most have small leaves that are tough and leathery. Small leaves **stand up to** cold and wind better than large leaves do. Some leaves are covered with soft little hairs. These tiny hairs **trap** water. They help keep tundra plants from drying out.

....

Run your fingers over Touch

stand up to survive

trap catch

A covering of tiny hairs helps keep the arctic poppy's leaves and stems from drying out.

The flower clusters of a least willow glow in the sun. Least willows are related to willow trees found in other biomes, but grow only a few inches to a foot high.

21

Bees carry pollen from flower to flower. With pollen, flowers make seeds.

Summers go by so quickly on the tundra that the plants must **hurry to grow**. As soon as the snow begins to melt at the end of winter, **green shoots pop up**. They sprout from seeds or roots that survive the long, cold months underground. As flowers begin to bloom, the tundra **explodes with color**. The plants must flower and make seeds before winter returns.

Small shrubs grow on the tundra, too. They don't die back to the ground at the end of summer, like flowers do. Instead, their woody stems grow a little bit each year. So don't be fooled by their small size. Many of these shrubs are older than your parents are.

An arctic ground squirrel feeds on the buds of a least willow shrub (above left). Yellow geum flowers attract bees and other insects with their bright petals (far left).

....

hurry to grow grow quickly
green shoots pop up little plants come out of the ground
explodes with color becomes very colorful

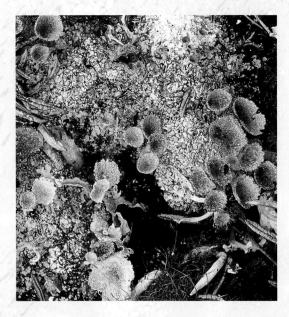

Lichens come in all shapes and sizes (left). Colorful lichens grow everywhere on the tundra—even on bare rock (below).

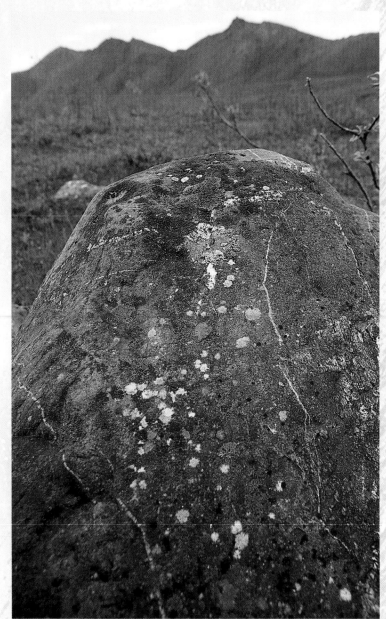

Lichens grow on the ground and on rocks. Some look like splashes and smears of orange, yellow, and black paint. Lichens are very tough. They can survive in the coldest, driest places, where nothing else can grow.

Green plants and colorful lichens are food for many tundra animals. Listen. Hear that **rustling** in the grass? It's a lemming. A lemming looks like a big short-tailed mouse.

....

rustling noise

Mother lemmings give birth to their babies in underground burrows.

It's about the size of your hand. Summer is a busy time for lemmings. They **scurry** from place to place, looking for grasses and seeds to eat.

The lemmings are also busy starting new families. Some summers, mother lemmings give birth to many babies. When that happens, the **lemming population gets** very, very large. Already this year, lemmings seem to be *everywhere* on the tundra.

A collared lemming looks for more plants to eat.

....

scurry run quickly
lemming population gets number of lemmings gets

BEFORE YOU MOVE ON...

1. **Cause and Effect** Reread page 16. Why does the ground become squishy in summer?

2. **Details** Reread pages 18–19. The main idea is: Plants don't grow well on the tundra. What are the details?

LOOK AHEAD How do animals survive on the tundra? Read pages 26–33 to find out.

25

If you look carefully, you might see some of the other animals that live on the arctic tundra **year-round**. An arctic hare **crouches** behind that clump of grass. You can just see the tips of its ears. It is hiding from an arctic fox. Arctic foxes are predators. Predators hunt and eat other animals.

An arctic hare, in its grayish brown summer coat, blends in with its background (above). But a hare whose white winter coat has not yet changed is easier for predators to see (right).

year-round all year
crouches hides

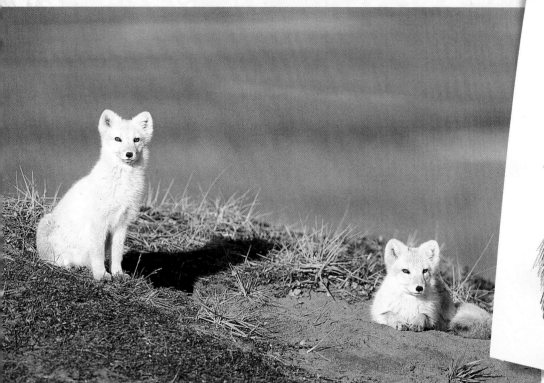

A fox's fur has two layers. Soft, fluffy underfur keeps in heat. Long, thick guard hairs block the wind.

Both arctic hares and arctic foxes have thick, fluffy coats of fur to keep them warm in the winter. These wonderful fur coats change color during the year. In summer, arctic hares and foxes have grayish brown fur that matches the rocks and soil. In winter, their coats become white, which **blends in with** the snow. Summer or winter, these animals **wear a perfect disguise**.

Arctic foxes, still in winter white, watch intently as something moves in the grass nearby.

....

blends in with is the same color as
wear a perfect disguise are hard to see

A ptarmigan's large outer feathers keep out wind and snow. Its inner down feathers are fluffy and trap heat.

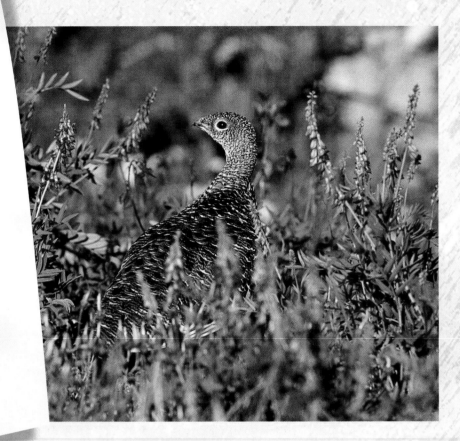

In her summer coat of spotted feathers, this ptarmigan blends into her surroundings. When she stands still, she is almost invisible.

The ptarmigan has a white coat in winter, too. But its coat is made of feathers. When summer comes, a ptarmigan grows feathers that **are spotted brown and gray**. A ptarmigan is resting among some wildflowers. You might not even notice her until she moves **out into the open** to look for seeds to eat. But when she does, she will be careful. She is being watched from the sky.

....

are spotted brown and gray have brown and gray spots
out into the open away from the flowers

Snowy owls soar over the tundra, **summer and winter**. These great white birds are **fierce predators**. They catch and eat ptarmigans, arctic hares, and even arctic foxes. But a snowy owl's favorite food is lemmings.

Snowy owl parents feed a lemming to their fluffy chicks.

summer and winter all year long
fierce predators good hunters

A pack of arctic wolves hunts together on the tundra.

Lemmings, hares, foxes, and ptarmigans all have to watch for even bigger predators. Arctic wolves **roam** the tundra, too. They live in family groups called packs.

And huge, powerful polar bears live along the tundra's edges, where land meets icy sea. Polar bears spend most of their time near the water, hunting seals. A polar bear is one animal

roam move around

you do *not* want to meet while walking across the tundra. Polar bears can run surprisingly fast and will eat anything they can catch.

A sleepy polar bear sniffs the breeze as he basks in the sun.

A young musk ox stays close to its mother while the herd wades across a stream.

Let's climb to the top of a low hill for a better view. Far off in the distance, you can see some of the strangest-looking **tundra residents**. Musk oxen are great, shaggy beasts with long hair that almost reaches the ground. They live in herds, like cattle. Their pointed, curved horns are good weapons against polar bears and wolves.

When **danger threatens**, musk oxen stand shoulder to shoulder in a line, facing their enemy. They lower their sharp horns, snort loudly, and **stomp their mighty hooves**. If they're

....

tundra residents animals living in the tundra
danger threatens an enemy comes near
stomp their mighty hooves step up and down

surrounded by a pack of arctic wolves, musk oxen will form a tight circle with their heads and horns pointing out. Their babies stay in the middle where it's safe.

When musk oxen are surrounded by wolves, they make a circle with their horns pointing out.

Grazing as he goes, a musk ox bull wades through tundra plants. His pointed horns are very sharp.

BEFORE YOU MOVE ON...

1. **Viewing** Reread page 27. How do the photos on page 26 help you understand the purpose of the hare's fur?

2. **Classify** Which animals are predators and which ones are prey?

LOOK AHEAD Read pages 34–39 to find out what comes to the tundra in the summer.

Summer visitors come to the tundra.
Plants bloom and insects buzz. Then plants
and animals prepare for winter again.

Caribou have big hooves
that keep them from
sinking into snow or
mushy wet ground.

Every year, when the snow begins to melt, other animals
arrive. These summer visitors move up from the south to spend
June, July, and August on the tundra. Caribou come in huge

A hungry caribou calf nurses while its mother watches for danger (above). A herd of caribou splash through a shallow river as they move across the tundra (left).

herds to eat the grasses and lichens. They also come to **give birth to their calves**. Do you see the caribou herd in the distance? Thousands and thousands of caribou move slowly over the treeless plain.

....

give birth to their calves have babies

A nest of eggs is well hidden.

With wings flapping, greater white-fronted geese descend on a shallow tundra lake. They will build their nests out of grass.

Most of the summer visitors are birds. Watch them **winging their way** across the sky. They come by the millions to build nests, lay eggs, and raise their chicks on the tundra.

Tundra swans honk loudly as they fly overhead. Crowds of geese and ducks and loons paddle across shallow lakes and build nests along the banks. A sandhill crane **strides about** on long legs. She's **on the lookout** for foxes and owls. Those predators would like to eat the crane's eggs, lying hidden in the grass.

Smaller birds, like redpolls and white-crowned sparrows, **flit from perch to perch**. They never fly far from their secret nests.

winging their way flying
strides about walks
on the lookout watching
flit from perch to perch move around a lot

Their hungry, **downy** chicks **huddle** in the nests, waiting for food.

And what do most tundra chicks eat? Insects! Shallow pools and damp ground are perfect places for all sorts of insects to lay their eggs. Clouds of **newly hatched** mosquitoes rise from lakes and ponds. Blackflies and gnats fill the air. Do you hear them buzzing and humming? Can you feel them crawling on your skin?

....

downy soft, feathered
huddle stay close together
newly hatched baby

*Mosquitos hatch in
pools of water.*

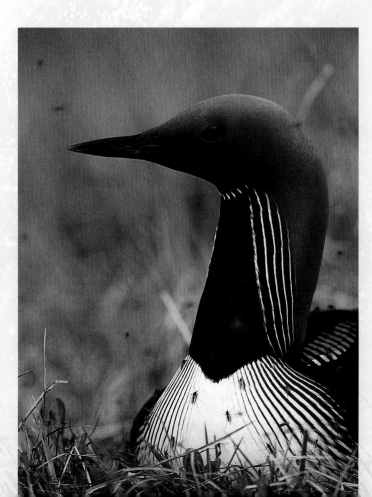

*Hungry mosquitos
swarm over a loon
as she sits on the
eggs in her nest.*

The mosquitoes and biting flies can be **ferocious**. But the **swarms** of insects are wonderful food for hungry baby birds. Mother and father birds fly through the air or walk in the grass, **snapping up** flies and bugs. Back at their nests, they stuff their catch into their chicks' **gaping** mouths. Then they quickly fly off again to gather the next meal.

....

ferocious mean
swarms large groups
snapping up eating
gaping open

A tundra swan swims with its two fluffy cygnets (left). Newly hatched Lapland longspur chicks wait in their nest for food (top). Nearby, their father has just caught a juicy insect (above).

The birds on the tundra work **day and night** to bring food to their chicks. They are racing against time. Summer will soon be over. Young birds must grow quickly. They must be ready to fly before the cold and darkness of winter return.

Other tundra babies are also growing fast under the midnight sun. Fox pups wrestle with each other. They try to catch lemmings in the grass. Caribou calves **scamper** and jump. Young musk oxen still **stick** close to their mothers. But they are getting stronger and bigger each day. Everywhere you look, the tundra is full of light and color and life.

day and night all the time
scamper run
stick stay

Arctic fox pups play hard and grow quickly.

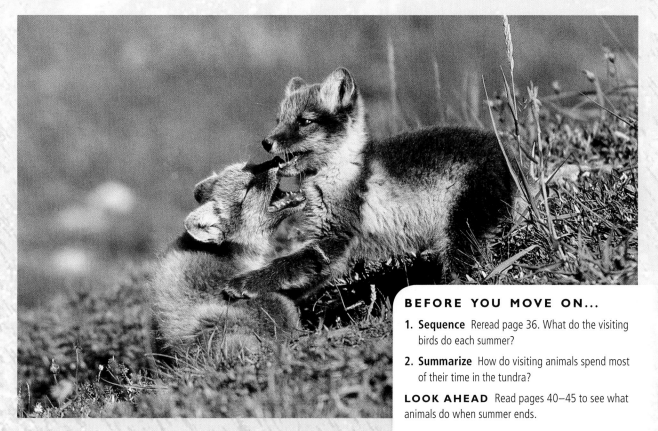

BEFORE YOU MOVE ON...

1. **Sequence** Reread page 36. What do the visiting birds do each summer?

2. **Summarize** How do visiting animals spend most of their time in the tundra?

LOOK AHEAD Read pages 40–45 to see what animals do when summer ends.

Seeds of most tundra
plants are small enough
to be scattered by the
wind. The arctic poppy
has very tiny seeds.

As winter approaches, the leaves of tundra plants, like the least willow, turn from green to gold, bronze, and scarlet (left). Ripe, ruby-red lingonberries (below) are eaten by arctic foxes and polar bears.

But it won't last long. Already, berries are getting ripe, and seeds are falling to the ground. In just a few weeks, the green color of the tundra plants disappears. The plants **put on their fall colors—fiery** reds, deep purples, and dark golds.

....

put on their fall colors change colors
fiery bright

41

As summer ends, caribou begin their journey south.

Near the end of August, the summer birds fly south to warmer places. **Flocks** of ducks and geese look like giant Vs **scrawled** across the sky.

The herds of caribou move south, too. They slowly **tramp** across the faded tundra, **nibbling** lichens as they go. The caribou spend the winter in the great forests south of the tundra. There, they are sheltered from the wind and can find enough food to eat.

....

Flocks Groups
scrawled written
tramp walk
nibbling eating

A ptarmigan's feathery "snowshoes" keep it from sinking into the snow.

The sun gets lower in the sky each day. Stinging cold winds blow down from the North Pole, bringing frost and then snow. The **blanket of snow** protects seeds and roots from the bitter cold.

By September, all the summer animals are gone. Only the **hardy** animals remain.

Thick coats of feathers and fur change from brown to white. The ptarmigan even grows feathers between its toes. Like snowshoes, these fluffy feathers help the ptarmigan walk on top of the snow.

In their white winter coats, ptarmigans puff their feathers against the cold wind.

The sun gets lower in the sky each day. There is less sunlight in winter.

blanket of snow layer of snow

hardy tough

Safe in tunnels beneath the snow, lemmings spend the winter nibbling on seeds and the roots of plants.

A mother polar bear and her cub brave bitter cold and blowing snow during the long winter.

Some tundra animals **sleep the winter away** in **underground burrows**. Lemmings stay awake. They scurry through their tunnels beneath the snow and snack on seeds and roots.

But many other animals have no place to hide from **winter's fury**. The musk oxen, foxes, and polar bears depend on thick

---

sleep the winter away sleep all winter
underground burrows holes in the ground
winter's fury the very cold weather

layers of fat and fur to survive the winter. They **brave** darkness, **subzero temperatures**, and howling winds for nearly nine months.

But eventually, the long, dark winter on the arctic tundra will end. After what seems like forever, the sun will return to glow again on the snowy owl's wings. And the tundra will be **bursting** with life once more.

....

brave stay strong in
subzero temperatures temperatures below zero degrees
bursting filled

An arctic fox uses its fluffy tail to keep its nose and feet warm.

A musk ox's breath freezes in the chill morning air of spring.

BEFORE YOU MOVE ON...

1. **Main Idea and Details** On pages 43–45, animals grow thick coats and go underground. Why?
2. **Author's Point of View** How do you think the author feels about the tundra? Give examples.

for further
Information
about the Tundra

Books

Brown, Fern G. *Owls*. New York: Franklin Watts, 1991.

Darling, Kathy. *Arctic Babies*. New York: Walker, 1996.

DuTemple, Lesley A. *Polar Bears*. Minneapolis: Lerner, 1997.

Fox-Davies, Sarah. *Little Caribou*. Cambridge, MA: Candlewick, 1997.

Matthews, Downs. *Arctic Foxes*. New York: Simon & Schuster, 1995.

Merrick, Patrick. *Loons*. Chanhassen, MN: Child's World, 2000.

Miller, Debbie S. *A Caribou Journey*. Boston: Little, Brown, 1994.

Parker, Barbara K. *North American Wolves*. Minneapolis: Carolrhoda, 1998.

Patent, Dorothy Hinshaw. *Polar Bears*. Minneapolis: Carolrhoda, 2000.

Rootes, David. *The Arctic*. Minneapolis: Lerner, 1996.

Souza, D. M. *What's a Lemming?* Minneapolis: Carolrhoda, 1998.

Steele, Philip. *Tundra*. Minneapolis: Carolrhoda, 1997.

Stone, Lynn M. *Sandhill Cranes*. Minneapolis: Lerner, 1997.

Wadsworth, Ginger. *Tundra Discoveries*. Watertown, MA: Charlesbridge, 1999.

Yolen, Jane. *Welcome to the Ice House*. New York: Putnam, 1998.

Web Sites

Alaska Department of Fish and Game— Just for Kids
http://www.state.ak.us/local/akpages/ FISH.GAME/geninfo/kids/kids.htm

The Alaska Department of Fish and Game has a site for children, with photographs and facts about the animals of the Alaskan tundra.

Animals of the Arctic
http://tqjunior.thinkquest.org/3500

This page for students includes information about animals of the arctic, related activities, and stories read by Native Alaskans.

Arctic National Wildlife Refuge
http://www.r7.fws.gov/nwr/arctic/

The U.S. Fish and Wildlife Service has a guide to the Arctic National Wildlife Refuge, with information about the animals, plants, and the area itself.

What's It Like Where You Live—
Tundra Page
http://mbgnet.mobot.org/sets/tundra/index.htm

This site, part of the Evergreen Project, provides information about the tundra for children. It features pages about weather on the tundra, plant and animal life, and an account of a student's visit to the tundra.

WWF Schools for Wildlife Celebrates the
Arctic
http://www.wwfcanada.org/wwfkids/arctic/index.html

The Canadian branch of the World Wildlife Federation has a site for children about the people and wildlife of the arctic. It features facts about species, threats to the arctic, and activities.

Photo Acknowledgments

B & C Alexander: p20 (moss clumps), p26 (white hare), p30; **Gary Braasch Photography:** cover, p6, p14, p15, p16 (both photos), p18, p20 (tiny campion flowers) (white anemone), p21, p22, p23, p24 (both photos), p38 (baby birds), p40, p41, p42; **Gary Schultz:** p7, p10, p11, p12, p27, p28, p31, p33, p34, p35, p36, p37, p38 (Tundra swan swims with two cygnets), (Lapland longspur father with insect in his mouth), p39, p43, p44, p45; **Gunther Matschke:** p4, p29; **Wildshot:** p9 (Mark Wilson), p25 (Mark Wilson), p26 (gray hare, Mark Wilson), p32 (Mark Wilson)

Index

Numbers in **bold** refer to photos and drawings.